Puzzlemania®
What's the Word?

HIGHLIGHTS PRESS

Honesdale, Pennsylvania

CONTENTS

When you finish a puzzle, check it off √.
Good luck, and happy puzzling!

Crosswords

Find-It Funnies

A-Mazing!

2

Hidden Pictures®

Brainteasers

Fill-In Fun

Crack the Code

Word Searches

Word for Words

The letters in **SUBMARINE** can be used to make many other words. Use the clues below to come up with some of them. A flightless bird, for example, might make you think of the word EMU. See how many of the others you can guess.

S U B M A R I N E

1. **A flightless bird** <u>E M U</u>

2. **You might ride to school in this** __ __ __ __

3. **A male sheep** __ __ __

4. **Farm building** __ __ __ __ __

5. **Not far** __ __ __ __

6. **Umbrella weather** __ __ __ __ __

7. **Horse hair** __ __ __ __

8. **A flashlight ray** __ __ __ __ __

9. **Subtraction sign** __ __ __ __ __ __

10. **Ambulance sound** __ __ __ __ __ __

11. **He or she works with a doctor** __ __ __ __ __ __

12. **1 is one** __ __ __ __ __ __ __

Illustrated by Wendy Wax

Zany Z Puzzle

Zowie! Three dozen words that contain the letter **Z** are on this page. They can fit in the grid just one way. Use the number of letters in each word to figure out where it might fit. Now, go zoom into the **Z** zone!

Word List

3 Letters
ZAP
~~ZOO~~

4 Letters
BUZZ
HAZY
JAZZ
MAZE
SIZE
ZEAL
ZERO
ZEST
ZITI

5 Letters
BLAZE
DIZZY
FIZZY
GRAZE
MAIZE
OZONE
PIZZA
PLAZA
TOPAZ
ZEBRA

6 Letters
BREEZE
DAZZLE
SIZZLE
SNEEZE
SNOOZE
WIZARD
ZENITH
ZIPPER

7 Letters
DRIZZLE
GAZELLE
HORIZON
PUZZLES
SQUEEZE

8 Letters
BLIZZARD
TWEEZERS

There is more than meets the eye in this comic book store. Can you find the hidden objects?

ax

ladle

sock

bow tie

kite

horseshoe

sailboat

tack

flashlight

wrench

olive

toothbrush

comb

ring

banana

golf club

envelope

leaf

pepper

hot dog

candle

baseball bat

loaf of bread

pennant

WHAT'S THE MEANING OF THIS?

Each of these clues will lead you to a word or a phrase. You just have to look at them in the right way. How many can you name?

1. MILLI1ON

2. ME REPEAT

3. WEAR / LONG

4. CA just SE

5. HEAD / HEELS

6. DANCE DANCE DANCE DANCE (surrounding *)

7. 1 (with O inside)

8. ROADS / ROADS / ROADS

Illustrated by Jim Steck

Weight a Second!

Emma weighs 78 pounds. She has to take three one-pound bowling pins across a bridge that will hold only 80 pounds. How can she do it? Follow each line from a letter to a blank space and write the letter in that space. When you are finished, you will have the answer.

G T E H J M E L U G

G

Illustrated by Mike Moran

Time to Rhyme

Grab a pencil; away you go.
It's time to use the rhymes you know.
Every clue has a rhyming hint,
About the word you need to print.
To start things off, we filled in one.
Now try the rest and have some fun!

Across

1. Baseball stick; rhymes with **cat**
3. Banana or apple; rhymes with **toot**
6. Opposite of yes; rhymes with **row**
7. A pronoun for a thing; rhymes with **pit**
9. A brief sleep; rhymes with **map**
12. Small child; rhymes with **lot**
14. Unit of weight; rhymes with **jam**
16. To cry hard; rhymes with **cob**
18. Worn around the neck; rhymes with **fly**
19. Icy flakes; rhymes with **grow**
21. Steal; rhymes with **job**
24. A part of the body; rhymes with **hear**
25. A pronoun like us; rhymes with **flea**
26. Opposite of stop; rhymes with **low**
29. A color name; rhymes with **queen**
30. A female chicken; rhymes with **ten**

Down

1. Use this to catch fish; rhymes with **skate**
2. Opposite of from; rhymes with **zoo**
3. A snake's tooth; rhymes with **bang**
4. Opposite of out; rhymes with **win**
5. A part of your foot; rhymes with **doe**
8. Throw a ball; rhymes with **gloss**
10. A type of museum; rhymes with **dart**
11. Two of a kind; rhymes with **hair**
13. A musical pitch; rhymes with **cone**
15. A cat sound; rhymes with **sea cow**
17. A type of snake; rhymes with **Noah**
20. A small bird; rhymes with **ten**
22. A vegetable; rhymes with **mean**
23. A breakfast food; rhymes with **leg**
27. Either ___; rhymes with **score**
28. An exclamation; rhymes with **no**

13

Scuba Time

You can make a big splash in this maze by finding the one path from START to FINISH. Once you've got it, write the letters you find along the route in the spaces below to answer the riddle. Ready, set, dive in!

Start

Y

S

H

E

A

M

Y

B

A

O

G

U

Y

O

F

F

U

W

How do you say good-bye to the ocean?

◯◯◯ ◯◯◯◯ !

Illustrated by Steve Skelton

Nice to See You!

Hi! We're glad you stopped by. We've hidden **22** ways to say hello in this grid. Look up, down, across, backwards, and diagonally to greet as many as you can.

Word List

AHOY
BONJOUR
BUENOS DIAS
GOOD DAY
GOOD MORNING
GOOD TO SEE YOU
GREETINGS
GUTEN TAG
HELLO
HEY
HI THERE
HIYA
HOLA
HOW ARE YOU?
HOW DO YOU DO?
HOWDY
JAMBO
KONICHIWA
QUE PASA?
SALUTATIONS
WHAT'S UP?
WIE GEHTS?

Y J A M B O M V G H T H B Y
B A W I H C I N O K E Y Y P
O K G H B O N J O U R Y E H
D C N I Y H O W D Y D H S O
U G I T E W H A T S U P N W
O U N H H E X H O S G J O A
Y T R E D O H I S E R W I R
O E O R B E L Y E E E I T E
D N M E L Y L A E Y E E A Y
W T D L A T E R Y A T G T O
O A O Y A D D O G I E U U
H G O B Y E H U U H N H L E
L R G A S A P E U Q G T A Y
B U E N O S D I A S S S S B

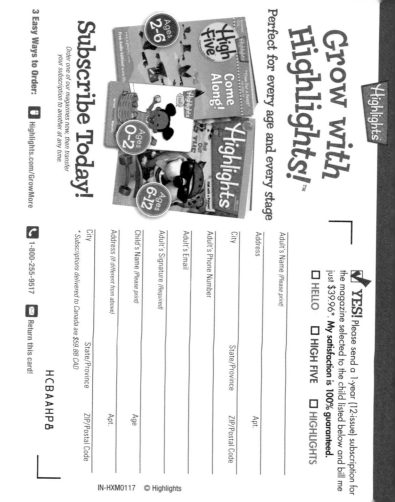

Grow with Highlights!™

Perfect for every age and every stage

Ages 2-6 — High Five — Come Along!
Ages 0-2 — Hello
Ages 6-12 — Highlights

☑ **YES!** Please send a 1-year (12-issue) subscription for the magazine selected to the child listed below and bill me just $39.96*. **My satisfaction is 100% guaranteed.**

☐ HELLO   ☐ HIGH FIVE   ☐ HIGHLIGHTS

Adult's Name *(Please print)*

Address _____ Apt. _____

City _____ State/Province _____ ZIP/Postal Code _____

Adult's Phone Number

Adult's Email

Adult's Signature *(Required)*

Child's Name *(Please print)* _____ Age _____

Address *(If different from above)* _____ Apt. _____

City _____ State/Province _____ ZIP/Postal Code _____

* Subscriptions delivered to Canada are $59.88 CAD

HCBAAHP8

Subscribe Today!

Order one of our magazines now, then transfer
your subscription to another at any time.

3 Easy Ways to Order:

📱 Highlights.com/GrowMore   📞 1-800-255-9517   ✉ Return this card!

IN-HXM0117   © Highlights

Double Cross

Puzzlemania's head chef, Pierre La Père, has come across a puzzling message in the pantry. To help Pierre find the answer to the riddle below, first cross out all the pairs of matching letters. Then write the remaining letters in order in the spaces beneath the riddle.

RR	AA	XX	BB	IT	CC	QQ
RI	ZZ	FF	TT	UU	ZZ	AA
VV	HH	AA	SE	WW	QQ	CC
JJ	OO	SA	LL	BB	FF	EE
DD	KK	PP	XX	EE	ND	RR
LL	SH	MM	NN	PP	RR	GG
II	IN	SS	VV	YY	EE	AA
SS	EE	CC	RR	ES	KK	FF

What does bread do when it is baked with shoe polish?

__ __ __   __ __ __ __ __   __ __ __   __ __ __ __ __ __

Ring the Bell

You can help Marcus ring the bell at the state fair. For each question, circle the answer listed under **A**, **B**, or **C**. Then shade in the matching square on the carnival bell ringer. As you do, the boxes will climb to the top. Can you guess whether column A, B, or C will ring the bell?

Which is ...

	A	B	C
1. a type of bread?	knickerbocker	pumpernickel	nickelodeon
2. where wool comes from?	goats	sheep	lions
3. the Valentine's Day month?	February	June	September
4. a leg bone?	radius	ulna	femur
5. what "smolder" means?	burn	shred	rush
6. a New England state?	California	Vermont	Kansas
7. the highest karate belt?	blue	green	black
8. a purple vegetable?	eggplant	zucchini	avocado
9. part of an atom?	automaton	krypton	neutron
10. a tooth?	incisor	razor	matador
11. the study of weather?	cometology	solarology	meteorology
12. a spicy food?	curry	slurry	jury
13. a basket material?	wicket	wicker	thistle
14. a primary color?	orange	yellow	brown
15. part of a comic strip?	committee	stanza	panel
16. a Canadian province?	Wales	Cape Town	Nova Scotia
17. a flower?	locus	lotus	locust
18. a giraffe's tongue color?	pink	black	orange
19. a tennis score of zero?	hug	kiss	love
20. a quick spin?	baguette	vignette	pirouette

19

From A to Z

Look around the scene. Find an item that starts with **A**, then one that starts with **B**, and so on until you've reached **Z**. Can you zero in on them all?

Hidden Pictures®
Alphabet Soup

glove

ring

crown

football

fish

wishbone

slice of pizza

envelope

teacup

mushroom

cane

hat

dog bone

crescent moon

Illustrated by Paula Becker

22

Sudoku Garden

Each of these grids holds a garden made up of just one type of flower. Fill in the boxes so that each row, column, and 6-letter section contains the letters of that flower. We've filled in some of the letters to get you started. Can you fill in the rest?

VIOLET

V	O	I	L	E	T
	L	E		I	O
	V			T	E
O	E		I		
	V	E	O		I
E	I			L	

ORCHID

H	D	C	O	R	I
		R	D		I
	H	I		O	D
	D		H		R
C				D	O
	R	O	H	I	

CLOVER

E	R	O	L	V	C
V		L			
			O		V
O			C		
R	V		E		O
L	O	E		C	R

Illustrated by Terry Taylor

Puzzle by Renee Heiss

23

HILARIOUS!

These hyenas have a serious case of the ha-has. They must be laughing at the funny words hidden in the grid on the next page. See how many you can find by looking up, down, across, backwards, and diagonally.

the grid on the next page

WORD LIST

~~ABSURD~~	JEST
AMUSE	JOKE
BIT	JOLLY
~~CACKLE~~	JOY
CHUCKLE	~~LAUGH~~
CLOWN	MIRTH
~~COMEDY~~	PRANK
FARCE	PUN
FROLIC	QUIP
FUN	RIDDLE
GAG	SKIT
GIGGLE	~~SMILE~~
GLEE	SMIRK
GRIN	STUNT
GUFFAW	~~TEE HEE~~
HA HA	TICKLE
HAPPY	~~ZANY~~
HILARITY	

24

V Q J O K E S K I T B W Y
P U H E L K C U H C I W P
U I T Y Y O J V Z E T O P
N P R K N A R P I L X H A
S M I L E A L E F K I J H
C O M E D Y Z L R C F U N
J P N W O L C D O I Y T S
E S U M A M G D L T E E T
S E A I J F Y I I G C E U
T L B J R E F R C A R H N
G G S C O E A U H G A E T
R G U X H L A U G H F E X
I I R Z I G L C A C K L E
N G D H O U I Y S M I R K

Illustrated by Ken Spengler

25

What's for BR3@kf@$+?

You never know what you will find at the **Password Diner**. Take a look at today's breakfast menu. Letters have been replaced by symbols and numbers. Can you figure out what's on today's menu?

BACON AND EGGS

B@©0n @nd 3gg$ _____

+0@$+3d 3ngl!$h muff!n _____

Blu3b3®®y p@n©@k3$ _____

W@ff13$ _____

0®@ng3 ju!©3 _____

0@+m3@l w!+h b®0wn $ug@® _____

Wh013 wh3@+ +0@$+ _____

F®3nch +0@$+ _____

©0ld ©3®3@l w!+h m!1k _____

$©®@mb13d 3gg$ _____

B@g31 w!+h ©®3@m ©h33$3 _____

V@n!11@ y0gur+ _____

©!nn@m0n ®011$ _____

H@$h b®0wn p0+@+03$ _____

B®3@kf@$+ bu®®!+0 _____

Box Drops

Each of these grids holds an **ocean riddle** and its punch line. To find out what the jokes are, you have to sort out the letters. Move the letters from each column into the boxes directly above them to form words. But be careful. The letters do not always go in the boxes in the same order as they appear. Each letter will be used only once. A black box means the end of a word. We've filled in some letters to get you started. Can you fill in the rest?

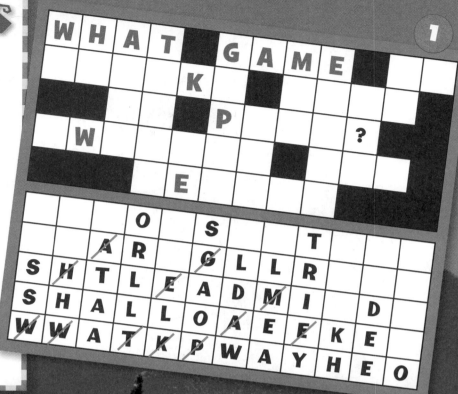

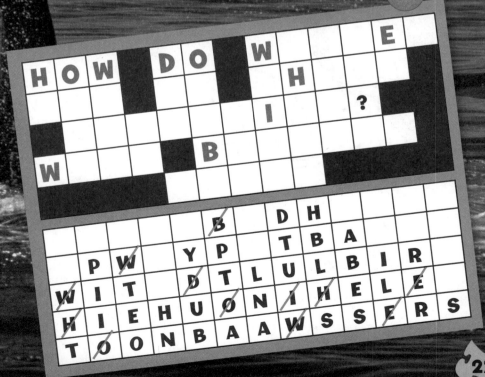

TRY 10

This quiz has 10 questions.
See how many you can get right.

1. Name three sports that start with B.

2. Name three words that rhyme with nice.

3. Circle the vegetable with the longest name.

4. If someone says, "Say cheese," what is probably about to happen?

5. The cheetah is the world's fastest land animal.
◯ True   ◯ False

6. "Museo" is the Spanish word for:
- music
- mustard
- museum

7. Can you think of two times you might say, "Excuse me"?

8. Name four countries.

10. Circle the vine with more leaves.

9. Mother's Day is in which month?
- March
- May
- July

29

Ready, Set, Grow!

This community garden is growing in popularity. Can you help Rosemary meet her friend Tom so they can water their plants? Just one path will take her there.

Start

S T R A M D T N T T P A

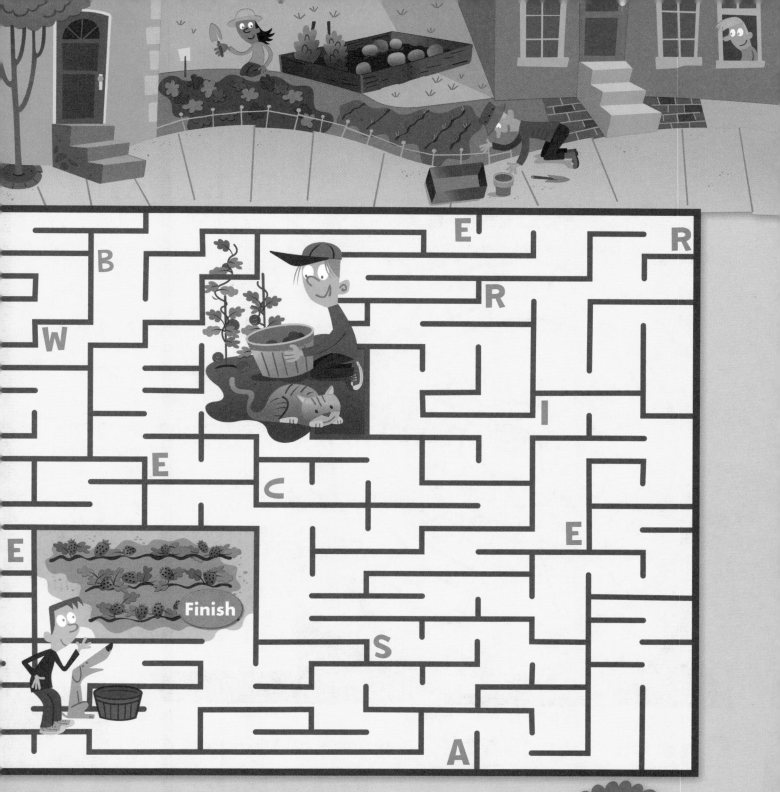

BONUS PUZZLE

Once you've found the correct path, write the letters along it in order in the spaces below. They'll answer this riddle:

What is a scarecrow's favorite fruit?

___ ___ ___ ___ ___ ___ ___ ___ ___ ___ ___

Illustrated by Jim Paillot

Game Q's

Go Seek!

Todd needs to find Agatha in this game of hide-and-seek. Can you help him find the one path to his friend?

Start

Fair Game

Here are four game sayings and their definitions. Can you guess which are true and which are false?

If someone has done work in advance, she is **ahead of the game.**

T or F

If someone **has got game**, it means he's not very talented.

T or F

If a store is **the only game in town**, it means it has mini-golf.

T or F

If someone has a **game plan**, he has a strategy in place.

T or F

Chess or Not?

Each pair of words has one chess piece and one faker. Circle the chess pieces.

Queen or Princess?

Kook or Rook?

Bishop or Cardinal?

Peon or Pawn?

Knight or Knave?

Jester or King?

Game Designer

Your friend is starting a board-game company and wants you to design the first game. Draw it here!

Missing Vowels

GM is the word *game* with the vowels taken away. Can you figure out the names of these five gms?

_____

TG

_____

HRSSHS

_____

HPSCTCH

_____

FLLW TH LDR

_____

CPTR TH FLG

A Pair of Jacks

Two of these jacks are exactly the same. Can you find the matching pair?

Puzzles by Carly Schuna

Illustrated by Mike Moran

33

Going in Circles

Around and around you'll go! Use the clues below to fill in the spaces on the next page. This is like a regular crossword puzzle, but with one twist: the last letter of each word will also be the first letter of the next word. Use those linking letters as hints to figure out the right words.

1. The tallest animal at the zoo
7. Opposite of exit
11. A large rodent
13. A king sits on one
18. Number of octagon sides
22. You hike on this
26. Midday meal
30. Snake sound
33. Kicking sport
38. A dried grape
43. Statue of Liberty state
49. First aid ____
51. Part of a BLT
56. Opposite of in
58. The Lone Star State
62. It makes cookies sweet
66. A baby shakes this
71. Macaroni shape
75. A color on the U.S. flag
79. Not difficult
82. The day before today
90. Opposite of old
94. "Farewell!"

G I R A F F E

All Talk

So you say you want a word search puzzle? It's good you spoke up! We've hidden **20** ways to say something in this grid. They are hiding up, down, across, backwards, and diagonally. How many can you find?

Word List

~~BABBLE~~
BELLOW
BLATHER
CRY
EXCLAIM
HISS
HOLLER
JABBER
MUMBLE
MURMUR

PRATTLE
PROCLAIM
RAMBLE
SCREAM
SCREECH
SHRIEK
SPEAK
WHISPER
WHOOP
YELL

```
S P E A K E T R E E I C
Z M U M B L E L L Y W S
S H H E D T X B B E O H
G Y H X W T B V M L L H
P R O C L A I M A L L H
H S L L B R S H R I E K
C C L A A P R M W W B B
E R E I B L A T H E R M
E E R M S H H O I C N C
R A M Q H Z O F S O R D
C M W I Q P V O P I S Y
S E S M J A B B E R H G
M S R U M R U M R E H D
```

Hidden Pictures®
Hieroglyphs

sock

artist's brush

hat

crown

banana

acorn

bell

crescent moon

comb

button

nail

golf club

tube of toothpaste

mug

toothbrush

cherry

ring

saltshaker

candle

Illustrated by Mike DeSantis

Good Fortune

Your fortune cookie has a coded message in it! Follow the directions below to crack the code and read your fortune.

```
_ _ _ _ _!  _ _ _   A           _ _ _
D J Y X G!  H P K  B̶ Q G  P T G

_ _   A     _ _   _ _ _ _ _ _!
D J  B̶ Q V  F P  P W Y G!
```

1. Change each **B** to the letter that comes before it in the alphabet.
2. Change the **X** to the letter that comes after **K** in the alphabet.
3. Each time you see a **Y**, change it to a letter that sounds like a part of the face.
4. Change each **Q** to a letter that sounds like the word *are*.
5. Change the **H** to the next-to-last letter of the alphabet.
6. Find a **T**. Change it to the letter that comes two letters before **P** in the alphabet.
7. Change each **D** to the letter that comes after **R** in the alphabet.
8. Change the **K** to a letter that sounds like the word *you*.
9. Change each **J** to the letter that comes three letters after it in the alphabet.
10. Change the **F** to a letter that sounds like the word *sea*.
11. Change the **V** to a letter that sounds like a hot drink.
12. Change the **W** to one of the letters in the word **OK**.
13. Change each **G** to the second vowel in the alphabet.
14. There should be four **P**'s remaining. Change each to a perfectly round letter to finish the message.

Just be yourself;
you are wonderful.

38

ANiMaL TRicKS

Each of these animals wants to change into a new one. Can you help them with this trick? Use the clues to fill in the blanks. Each word is only one letter different from the word above it. If you can solve all four, you have the magic touch!

1.

	C	A	T
A bed that folds up	__	__	__
The letter "i" has one	__	__	__
	D	O	G

2.

	W	O	R	M
I __ this shirt yesterday.	__	__	__	__
It carries electricity.	__	__	__	__
Smart like an owl	__	__	__	__
A want or desire	__	__	__	__
	F	I	S	H

3.

	G	O	A	T
It surrounds a castle.	__	__	__	__
Low sound of pain	__	__	__	__
Earth's satellite	__	__	__	__
A water bird	__	__	__	__
	L	I	O	N

4.

	D	U	C	K
A parking place for a boat	__	__	__	__
It keeps your foot warm.	__	__	__	__
To sit in a bath	__	__	__	__
To fly like an eagle	__	__	__	__
A mark left after a cut heals	__	__	__	__
Copy into a computer	__	__	__	__
	S	W	A	N

Illustrated by Pablo Bernasconi

39

Can you find the hidden objects that start with GR?

griddle

gravy boat

greeting card

grub

grapefruit

grasshopper

granola bar

graham cracker

grapes

grater

Illustrated by John Nez

Stop, Look, and List

Are you ready for a trivia challenge? Fill in each box with a name or word. It must begin with the letter at the top of the column. We put in a few of our favorites to get you started.

	S	T	O	P
Boys' Names				
Sandwich Ingredients			Onions	
Words with LL in Them	Silly			
Halloween Costumes				
Silly Ice-Cream Flavors		Taco Chip		
Birds				Penguin
Cities				
Baseball Words		Triple		

Scrambled Birds

Why do hummingbirds hum?
To find out, unscramble the bird
names below. Then write the numbered
letters in the answer spaces at the bottom
of the page.

DEVO — <u>D</u> <u>O</u> <u>V</u> <u>E</u>
12

CORW — _ _ _ _
8

WKAH — _ _ _ _
5

NASW — _ _ _ _
9

BINOR — _ _ _ _ _
2

RKOST — _ _ _ _ _
11

SOOGE — _ _ _ _ _
7

PEIGON — _ _ _ _ _ _
10

TORRAP — _ _ _ _ _ _
4

ASPRRWO — _ _ _ _ _ _ _
13

UPENING — _ _ _ _ _ _ _
3

GLOMIFAN — _ _ _ _ _ _ _ _
6

LARDCINA — _ _ _ _ _ _ _ _
1

Because they _ _ _ _ _ _ _ _ the _ _ _ _ <u>D</u> _ .
1 2 3 4 5 6 7 8   9 10 11 12 13

Cut It Out!

Gus was cutting the lawn when his mower got away from him. Can you help Gus catch up to his mower? Just one path will take you there.

Start

R

B

C

A

C

E

A

Y

S

S

R

R

A

BONUS PUZZLE

Once you've found the correct path, write the letters along it in order in the spaces below. They'll answer this riddle:

What do fishermen plant in their lawns?

◯ ◯ ◯ ◯ ◯ ◯ ◯ ◯ ◯

Illustrated by Steve Skelton

Finish

45

SwEEt!

Take a closer look. There are at least **40** things whose names contain the letters **EE**. How many do you see?

GENERAL STORE

COMPOST

47

Kiddie Ride

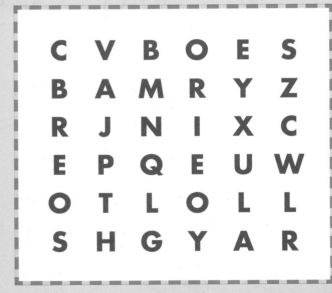

What do babies ride at amusement parks? To find out, follow the directions below. Each sentence will tell you where one letter is in the grid. Once you've found it, write it in the correct space or spaces below the riddle.

1. This letter is the first vowel in the top row.

2. This letter is two below the **J**.

3. Find the letter between a **Q** and a **U**.

4. This is the next-to-last letter in the bottom row.

5. This letter appears three times in the fifth row.

6. Find the letter that is directly above the **W**.

7. This letter is three above an **S**.

8. This letter is in two of the four corners.

C	V	B	O	E	S
B	A	M	R	Y	Z
R	J	N	I	X	C
E	P	Q	E	U	W
O	T	L	O	L	L
S	H	G	Y	A	R

What do babies ride at amusement parks?

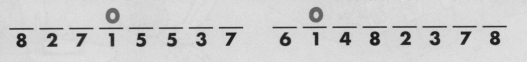

$\dfrac{}{8}\ \dfrac{}{2}\ \dfrac{}{7}\ \dfrac{O}{1}\ \dfrac{}{5}\ \dfrac{}{5}\ \dfrac{}{3}\ \dfrac{}{7}\qquad \dfrac{}{6}\ \dfrac{O}{1}\ \dfrac{}{4}\ \dfrac{}{8}\ \dfrac{}{2}\ \dfrac{}{3}\ \dfrac{}{7}\ \dfrac{}{8}$

Illustrated by Kelly Kennedy

Hidden Pictures®
Chinatown

Illustrated by Laura Ferraro Close

paper airplane

knitted hat

four-leaf clover

flower

pennant

tadpole

ladle

cane

whale

crescent moon

jellyfish

banana

lollipop

ring

drinking straw

49

X Marks the Spot

Can you feel the eXcitement? We've listed **35** words that contain the letter **X**. They fit into the grid in just one way. Use the number of letters in each word as a clue to where it might fit. Fill them all in, and you're eXceptional in our book!

3 letters
AXE
BOX
FOX
SIX

4 letters
EXAM
EXIT
FLEX
NEXT
OXEN
TAXI
TEXT
X-RAY

5 letters
EXACT
EXTRA
HELIX
RELAX
TEXAS
XENON

6 letters
EXCESS
EXCUSE
EXHALE
EXPECT
MEXICO

7 letters
EXHIBIT
EXPLORE
EXPRESS
EXTREME
MAXIMUM
TEXTILE

9 letters
EXCELLENT
EXCURSION
SAXOPHONE
XYLOPHONE

10 letters
EXPERIMENT

13 letters
EXTRAORDINARY

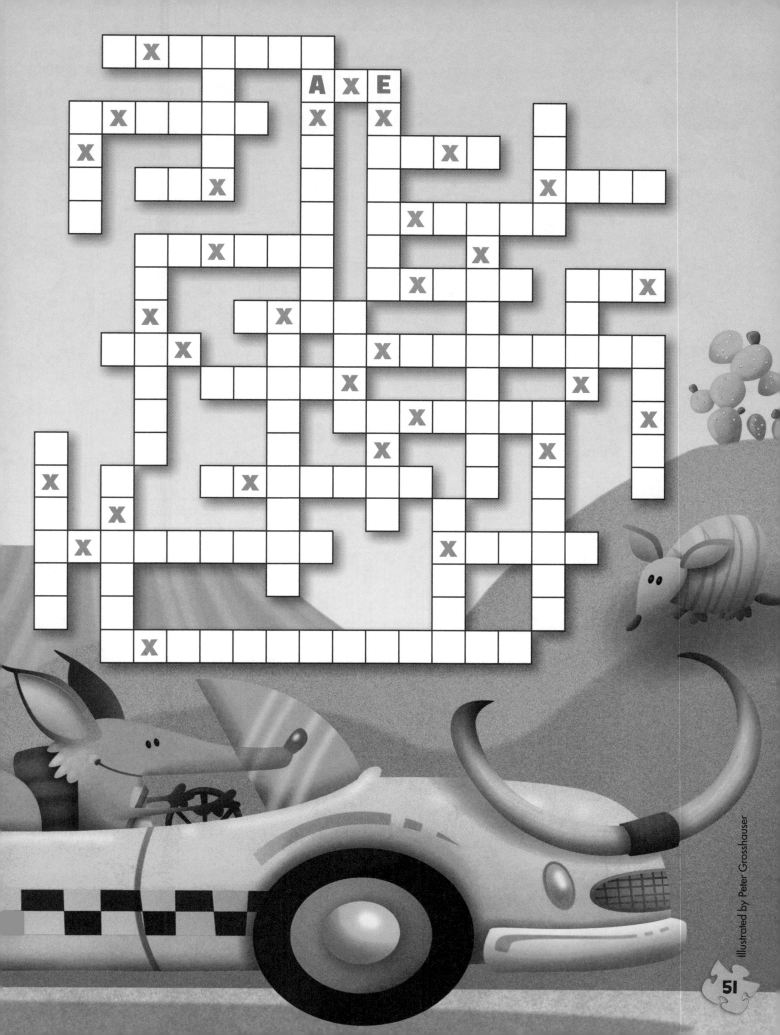

Hidden Pictures®
Metro Map

This city scene has many things to look for. Can you find the hidden objects?

umbrella

clamshell

game piece

paper clip

ring

lightning bolt

tuning fork

T square

52

hedgehog

hockey stick

domino

hanger

sailboat

earmuffs

pinecone

banana

fishhook

slice of pizza

paper plane

horseshoe crab

light bulb

bicycle pump

whistle

ruler

hot dog

crescent moon

clamp

rocket

wishbone

adhesive bandage

ice skate

trowel

spoon

saw

horn

rowboat

Illustrated by Mark Corcoran

53

Wh@+'s f0® lun©h?

You never know what you will find at the **Password Diner**. Take a look at today's lunch menu. Letters have been replaced by symbols and numbers. Can you figure out today's soups and sandwiches?

SOUPS

F®3n©h 0n!0n _____ FRENCH ONION _____

B33f B@@r13y _____

©h!©k3n N00d13 _____

©1@m ©h0wd3® _____

©®3@m 0f Mu$h®00m _____

$p1!+ P3@ w!+h H@m _____

SANDWICHES

B@©0n, 13++u©3, @nd +0m@+0 _____

3gg $@1@d _____

G®!113d ©h33$3 _____

H@m @nd ©h33$3 _____

P3@nu+ Bu++3® @nd J311y _____

Pu113d P0®k _____

®0@$+ B33f _____

+un@ M31+ _____

+u®k3y ©1ub _____

55

Catch You Later!

Word List

There are **33** ways to say good-bye hidden in this grid. How many can you find? Look up, down, across, backwards, and diagonally. Off you go! Bye now!

A RIVEDERCI
ADIEU
ADIOS
AU REVOIR
AUF WIEDERSEHEN
BE SEEING YOU
BON VOYAGE
BONJOUR
BYE-BYE
CHEERIO
CHEERS
CIAO
FAREWELL
GOOD-BYE
GOOD DAY
GOOD NIGHT
HAPPY TRAILS

HASTA LA VISTA
HAVE A NICE DAY
LATER
OVER AND OUT
PEACE
PIP-PIP
REGARDS
ROGER
SAYONARA
SEE YOU LATER
SHALOM
SO LONG
TAKE CARE
TAKE IT EASY
TA-TA
TOODLE-OO

Illustrated by Peter Grosshauser

```
E C A E P B O N V O Y A G E B
S E E Y O U L A T E R E O V O
H H R Z G G O O E L D O O T N
A I S O N G O O D D A Y D A J
L G X O G S G I A T Y Q B U O
O O L H I E A T R A A A Y F U
M O L P S E R U I K D U E W R
S D L J D S A O V E E R P I U
T N E T R F N D E I C E I E O
A I W E A K O N D T I V P D Y
K G E S G T Y A E E N O P E G
E H R B E I A R R A A I I R N
C T A S R F S E C S E R P S I
A E F C I A O V I Y V E S E E
R E T A L H I O A H A E O H E
E B B Y E B Y E O I H H I E S
H A P P Y T R A I L S C D N E
R H A S T A L A V I S T A H B
```

Flower Power

This petal puzzle works just like a normal crossword, except you work clockwise or counterclockwise. Each clue matches a numbered petal. Start your answer at the number and work toward the center of the flower. We've done both answers for petal 1 to get you started.

Buzzzzzzzz...

Clockwise

1. Dirt
2. You do this on a phone
3. A pretty flower with thorns
4. A little wet
5. A rake, hammer, or shovel
6. A single bit of rain
7. ____ on the cob
8. A type of fish; rhymes with sharp
9. They help with weeding.
10. A red root vegetable
11. Chaser of the three pigs
12. A group of ballplayers
13. Beef and pork
14. To loan
15. A feathered flyer
16. To install on a computer
17. Gardener's enemy
18. Lima, kidney, or string

Counterclockwise

1. A plant's beginning
2. Froglike creature
3. Water from the sky
4. Barbie or Raggedy Ann
5. Small job
6. Rounded building top
7. A field's yield
8. Chilled
9. Stringed instrument
10. Your birthday marks the day you were ____.
11. A word that means "to cry"
12. You have five on each foot
13. What ice will do in the sun
14. Food-making part of a plant
15. A flashlight sends a ____ of light.
16. Clothes dryer's fuzzy leftovers
17. Each answer in this puzzle is one ____.
18. Part of a necklace

Double Cross

To find the "purr-fect" answer to the riddle below, first cross out all the pairs of matching letters. Then write the remaining letters in order in the spaces beneath the riddle.

AA	TT	II	TH	SS	QQ	EY
HH	OO	BB	RR	AL	EE	VV
LH	NN	ZZ	YY	CC	AV	AA
II	QQ	EE	EN	DD	PP	WW
IN	GG	LL	TT	VV	EL	ZZ
XX	HH	IV	II	BB	OO	SS
TT	UU	NN	EE	SS	ES	MM

Why are cats good at video games?

THEY ALL HAVE NINE LIVES.

See You Later, Galilator

The head zookeeper at the World Zoo is done for the day. He must be tired, because when he said good-bye to the animals, he scrambled their names. Can you help straighten out each animal's name? When you do, each name will rhyme with the zookeeper's good-bye phrase. For example, a few minutes ago, he tried to say, "See you later, alligator."

1. After a while, DOCCOREIL _____

2. See you soon, you big NABBOO _____

3. Got to go, FABFULO _____

4. Time to sleep, bighorn PEESH _____

5. Cheerio, KECGO _____

6. Bye-bye, FEBLUTTRY _____

7. Toodle-oo, AKNARGOO _____

8. Take good care, RAPLO EBAR _____

9. That's all for me, PENCHEZAMI _____

10. Take a break, TRANTELSAKE _____

Puzzle by Cindy Blobaum

Illustrated by Dave Clegg

Fantastic Gymnastics

It's the day of the big tumbling competition. Can you help Maura with her routine? First, find the one path that goes from START to FINISH. Then use the letters you find along the path to answer the riddle.

Start

G

E

A

U

E

O

D

H

U

I

C

E

U

A

How do gymnasts feel after a routine?

Everything Is OK!

O, say can you see . . . a kangaroo? What about an owl? This scene is filled with things that start with the letters O and K. See if you can find at least 25 words that begin with an O or a K.

64

Illustrated by Tim Haggerty

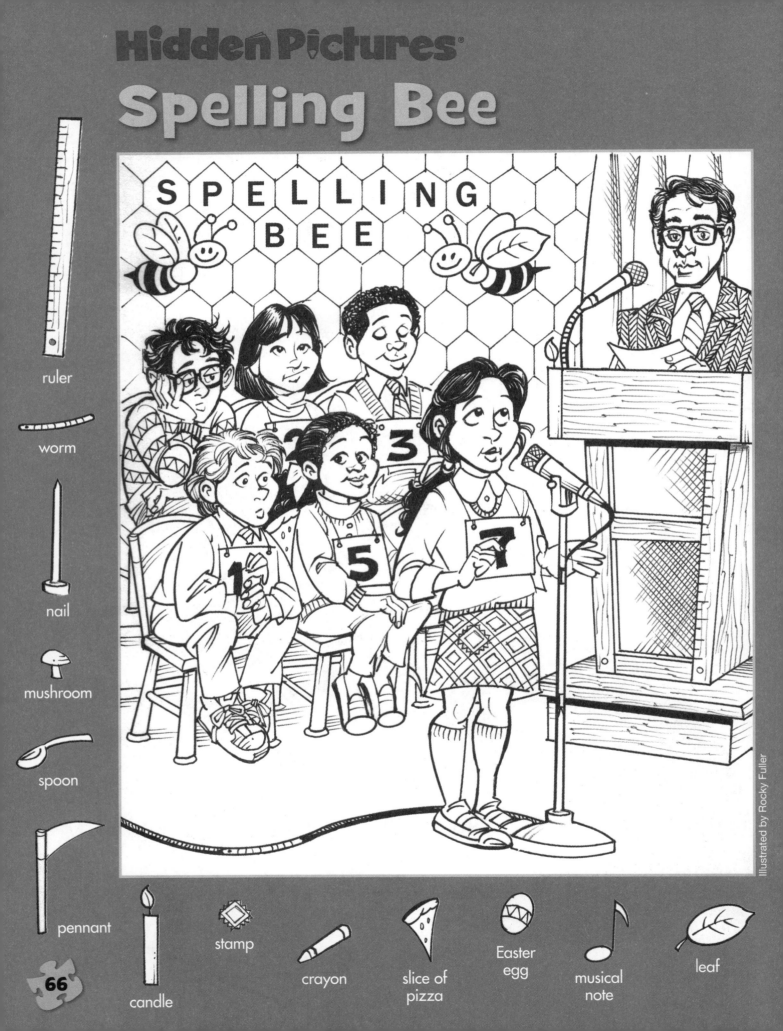

Hidden Pictures®
Spelling Bee

ruler

worm

nail

mushroom

spoon

pennant

candle

stamp

crayon

slice of pizza

Easter egg

musical note

leaf

66

Mixed Nuts Sudoku

You'll go nuts for this puzzle! Each grid holds one type of nut. Fill in the boxes so that each row, column, and 6-letter section contain the letters of that nut. We've filled in some of the letters to get you started. Can you fill in the rest?

ALMOND

A	L	M	O	N	D
	O	N		M	A
	A				L
O	M		D		
		A	N	L	O
L	N		D		

PEANUT

P	E	A	N	U	T
T		U		N	U	T
			E		U
E			A		
N	T		U		A
U	A	E		N	P

CASHEW

C	A	S	H	E	W
	H	A			
W	H			C	E
	E			A	
A				H	S
	S	C	E	W	

67

Eek!

Take a peek at this puzzle. There are **33** words hidden in the grid that rhyme with *eek*. Look for them up, down, across, backwards, and diagonally. Can you find them all? Go seek!

Word List

~~ANTIQUE~~	PEEK
BATIK	PIQUE
BEAK	SEEK
BOUTIQUE	SHEIK
CHEEK	SHRIEK
CHIC	SLEEK
CLIQUE	SNEAK
CREAK	SPEAK
CREEK	SQUEAK
CRITIQUE	STREAK
FREAK	TEAK
GREEK	TECHNIQUE
LEAK	TWEAK
MARTINIQUE	UNIQUE
MEEK	WEEK
MOZAMBIQUE	WREAK
MYSTIQUE	

```
K A B O U T I Q U E K R X C S
C K E E R C M H S E P S K R U
G I C C L I Q U E K E T A E G
S K H J J B A H U O E R E A K
H A A C R A C X K V K E P K P
E E E E M T F R E A K A S D I
I R U U T I G P E G B K E Y Q
K W Q Q K K T G R K A E N S U
S B I I S A W P G U N I Q U E
L A N T Q B E U Q I T N A K K
E N H S U K A L V K U F V E Q
E Q C Y E F K K Z S H R I E K
K E E M A R T I N I Q U E W Q
S Z T I K M O Z A M B I Q U E
C R B E A K U E U Q I T I R C
```

Do the Opposite

Some of the answers to this crossword are opposites. Use the clues to fill in as much of the grid as you can. Time to get started. Are you in or out?

Across

1. Opposite of happy
4. Opposite of on
6. Opposite of the truth; a lie
8. The month after April
10. 2,000 pounds
11. Opposite of older
14. You and me
15. A laughing word
16. Spanish for one
17. Opposite of Ma
18. Abbreviation for South Dakota
20. Flew a plane
23. A basketball hoop has one.
24. ____ and then
26. Opposite of cold
27. Opposite of wet
28. A jewel

Down

2. "I ___ here."
3. Opposite of night
5. It blows cool air.
6. Opposite of against
7. Opposite of out
9. "How are ____ doing?"
10. A drink served hot or iced
12. Normal, regular
13. Halloween costume made from a sheet
17. A peach's center
19. A fox's home
20. A cat, hamster, or goldfish, perhaps
21. You row a boat with this.
22. A Dalmatian or a poodle
23. Opposite of yes
25. You and me

Illustrated by Kelly Kennedy   Puzzle by Donna L. Huisjen

Each grid holds the beginning to a familiar song. To find out what the songs are, you have to sort out the letters. Move the letters from each column into the boxes directly above them to form words. But be careful. The letters do not always go in the boxes in the same order as they appear. Each letter will be used only once. A black box means the end of a word. We've filled in some letters to get you started. Can you fill in the rest?

Box Drops

72

A Tree Stumper

Ten types of trees are hiding in the scrambled letters below. Can you figure out the name of each? We did the first one to get you started. "Wood" you do the rest? When you're done, the circled letters will tell you the name of the tallest species of tree in the world.

LAWTUN	W A L N U (T)
RYRECH	_ (O) _ _ _ _
NIPE	_ _ _ (O)
CHRIB	_ _ (O) _ _
PLEAM	_ _ _ _ (O)
RACED	_ _ (O) _ _
OWLWIL	(O) _ _ _ _ _
KOA	(O) _ _
ROCKYHI	_ _ _ _ _ (O) _ _
GOODWOD	_ _ _ _ _ _ (O)

The world's tallest species of tree is

(T) ◯ ◯   ◯ ◯ ◯ ◯ ◯ ◯ ◯ .

Puzzle by Lori Mortensen

73

Flowers and Flamingoes

Can you find the hidden objects that begin with FL?

flying saucer

flashlight

flying fish

flea collar

flour sack

flash card

flag

flute

flip-flop

flyswatter

Illustrated by John Nez

75

Pizza Path

Parker is meeting his friends at the busiest pizzeria in town. They've saved him a seat, but he needs to figure out how to get there. Can you help Parker find the one path to his friends?

Bonus Puzzle

Once you've found the correct path, write the letters along it in order in the spaces below. They'll answer this question:

Parker does not like salt. So what will he order on his pizza?

_ _ _ _ _ _ _ _ _ _ _

Illustrated by Ron Zalme

SHHHHHHHH!

Listen up! There are **32** noisy things hidden in this grid. Look (and listen) for them up, down, across, backwards, and diagonally. Now go see what all the racket is about.

Word List

APPLAUSE

BAGPIPES

BARKING DOG

BUGLE

BULLHORN

CAR HORN

CHAINSAW

CRYING BABY

DRILL

DRUMS

ELECTRIC GUITAR

FIRE ALARM

FIREWORKS

FOGHORN

GONG

JACKHAMMER

JET ENGINE

LION'S ROAR

MARCHING BAND

MOTORCYCLE

MOWER

NOISEMAKER

ROLLER COASTER

SCREAM

SIREN

SNORING

SUBWAY

THUNDER

TORNADO

TRAIN

VACUUM

WHISTLE

```
W I M O T O R C Y C L E X T W L
( A P P L A U S E ) B I N Q T H E L
S Q U I E T S N O R I N G U L M
N E S U B W A Y O S H H R N E A
I E N Z C A R H O R N T O D C R
A J R I C E L T S I H W L E T C H
H A E F G L D R U M S B L R R H I
C C W X U N S C R E A M E A I I
R K O B Y E E D U R C N R O C N
Y H M N I A R T K I A R C R G G
I A D R I L L I E T L O O S U B
N M P E E P N E D J M H A N I A
G M V B A G P I P E S G S O T N
B E Q A D W O D A N R O T I A D
A R A O C G O N G H W F E L R R
B U G L E U S K R O W E R I F K
Y N E R I S U F I R E A L A R M
R Z N O I S E M A K E R H U S H
```

79

Illustrated by Peter Grosshauser

Q Cross

Here's a quirky crisscross quest for you. We've gathered **18** words that contain the letter **Q**. They fit into the grid in just one way. Use the number of letters in each word as a clue to where it might fit.

5 Letters	6 Letters	7 Letters	8 Letters
QUAIL	QUAINT	ANTIQUE	FREQUENT
QUIET	QUENCH	AQUATIC	QUESTION
QUILT	SQUASH	LACQUER	
SQUID	UNIQUE	QUALIFY	
		QUARREL	
		QUARTER	
		QUIBBLE	
		SQUELCH	

Hidden Pictures
Teaching T

Ms. Toffy is tackling words that begin with the letter *T*. Can you find the hidden objects that start with *T*?

DEFGHIJKLMNOPQRS

tiger   top
termite   trout
telescope   toboggan
trench   toe
toucan   toad
twirl   tickle
tangle

teardrop

toaster

tooth

teacup

trumpet

tennis racket

tube

tweezers

tomato

teapot

toothbrush

tack

top hat

turtle

tent

Illustrated by Paula Becker

Strange!

There are some strange things going on in this St scene. Take a closer look at it. There are at least **30** things whose names begin with the letters St. How many can you find?

TBONE'S

TBONE'S RESTAURANT

DINO'S DINER

FIRST STREET SCHOOL

Illustrated by James Yamasaki

82

T Party

Ta-da! This is one terrific puzzle. All of the answers to these clues start with the letter *T*. We've added the *T*'s at the start of each word. Can you figure out the rest? Take a try.

Across

1. Opposite of bottom
3. Use this to look at stars.
4. The _____ Fairy
5. The Lone Star State
7. Opposite of loose
9. The main dish at a Thanksgiving dinner
10. Venus and Serena Williams's sport
11. You set this with place mats.
12. A day of the week
13. A healthy food made from soy beans
14. An elephant has one.
15. One of the five senses
19. Sleepy
20. Drink it hot or iced.
21. A score in football

Down

1. "_____ peas in a pod"
2. To heat a slice of bread
3. Number of eggs in a baker's dozen
4. Neat and clean
5. A funnel-shaped storm
6. What you might yell as you're cutting down a tree
8. A three-wheeled bike
10. Elm or maple
11. Where you put deleted items on the computer
12. "Rub-a-dub-dub, three men in a _____"
13. A pickup or an eighteen-wheeler
14. Not false
15. What a clock tells
16. The T in BLT
17. "_____ or treat!"
18. A crisp tortilla with filling

Illustrated by Peter Grosshauser

Puzzle by Carly Schuna

Fish Tales

kite

ghost

button

lollipop

pliers

heart

crescent moon

slice of watermelon

fried egg

86

Illustrated by Ellen Appleby

comb

carrot

flower

snake

worm

artist's brush

envelope

What's the Word?

Puzzlemania's Online Dictionary has gone haywire. Can you help us straighten out these definitions? Circle the one that answers each question.

1. Is a **PANINI** a type of sandwich or a clown?

2. Is a **POLLYWOG** a tadpole or a shape with many sides?

3. Is a **FROCK** a group of sheep or a dress?

4. Is a **MINNOW** a type of car or a small fish?

5. Is a **MARINA** a place to dock boats or a type of spaghetti sauce?

6. Is a **CYGNET** a ring or a baby swan?

7. Is a **DOLLOP** a small portion or a kind of lollipop?

8. Is an **ANACONDA** a snake or an airplane?

9. Is a **QUETZAL** a kind of instrument or a bird?

10. Is a **ZIGGURAT** a type of painting or an ancient pyramid?

Illustrated by Wendy Wax

87

Swim Meet

Kiera wants to meet her friend at the far end of the pool.
Can you find the one path that will take her there?

Start

BONUS PUZZLE

Did you find the path? Now write all the letters you found on it, in order, in the spaces below. They'll answer the riddle.

Where do minivans go swimming?

___ ___ ___   ___ ___ ___ ___ ___

Illustrated by Ron Zalme

89

Word for Words

The letters in **UMBRELLAS** can be used to make many other words. Use the clues below to come up with some of them. Body of water, for example, might make you think of the word SEA. See how many of the others you can guess.

1. **Body of water** <u>S E A</u>

2. **A way to get to school** __ __ __ __

3. **You ring it** __ __ __ __

4. **The Red Planet** __ __ __ __

5. **Lunch or dinner** __ __ __ __

6. **It bounces** __ __ __ __

7. **Grizzly or polar** __ __ __ __

8. **You hear with them** __ __ __ __

9. **Donkey** __ __ __ __

10. **Navy color** __ __ __ __

11. **Opposite of different** __ __ __ __

12. **Use your nose** __ __ __ __ __

13. **Piece of wood** __ __ __ __ __

14. **Opposite of bigger** __ __ __ __ __ __

15. **Small, round glass toys** __ __ __ __ __ __ __

Illustrated by Eldon Doty

A Key Clue

These puzzle pirates have found the treasure chest, but they will need your help to open it. As you decipher the secret message, put the last letter of each word first and the first letter last. As you do, you will tell the pirates what they need to know.

You must
uoy tusM HedRcS eHt dsLaNi. DiNf eivf
Seyk NiddeH Ni eHt eictuRP. yHet LiLw
NPeo eHt sockL No eHt eReasURt tHEsc.

Illustrated by Jim Paillot

Up aNd Down

Are you up for this puzzle? We've put **40** words down in this grid that contain the letters UP or DOWN. Each time UP appears in a word, it is replaced by a ⬆. And each time DOWN appears in a word, it is replaced by a ⬇. Look across, backwards, diagonally, and, of course, up and down, to find the words.

Word List

~~BACKup~~
BREAKdown
BREAKup
BUILDup
CHECKup
CLOSE-up
downBEAT
downFALL
downHEARTED
downHILL
downLOAD
downPLAY
downPOUR
downRIVER
downSLIDE
downSTAIRS
downTRODDEN
HOEdown
LOWdown
MAKEup

MELTdown
PULL-up
ROUNDup
SHAKEup
SHUTdown
SIT-up
SPLASHdown
SUNdown
TOUCHdown
WARM-up
WINDup
upDATE
upKEEP
upROAR
upROOT
upSET
upSIDE down
upSTAIRS
upSTART
upTURN

93

B ALL YOU CAN B

This puzzle is bound to **B** a bunch of fun. All of the answers to these clues start with the letter **B**. We've added the **B**'s at the start of each word. Can you figure out the rest? Ready, set, **B**-gin!

Across

1. Largest country in South America
2. Make this from soap or gum.
5. These straighten teeth.
6. A panda's favorite food
8. A janitor might push this.
9. Good, _____, best
11. Spread cream cheese on it.
13. Celebrate this with cake and candles.
14. Hot-air _____
15. First meal of the day
18. A game with a hoop
20. A groom's partner
21. What a majorette twirls

Down

1. Do this on a trampoline.
2. Capital of Massachusetts
3. A place to build a sandcastle
4. A library has many of these.
5. Home city to the Ravens and the Orioles
7. Monarch or swallowtail
8. Meal between 15 Across and lunch
9. Piggy _____
10. Baked chocolate treat
12. Slice this on cereal.
13. Stomach
14. Wrist jewelry
16. Type of dance with tutus and toe shoes
17. Sound a dog makes
18. Hamburger or steak
19. A horse's home

Illustrated by Peter Grosshauser

TRY 10

1. Circle the fifth letter of the alphabet.

E G k

2. How many inches are in two feet?
○ 12 ○ 24 ○ 100

3. Name two animals that have spots.

4. How many months begin with the letter J?

5. In which state can you see the Alamo?
○ Alabama ○ Nevada ○ Texa

6. Name three words that rhyme with "oat."

7. Name three things you can make using apples.

8. Circle the letter with the stamp in the correct place.

9. The Spanish word "beisbol" means bubble.
○ True ○ False

10. Name two things that are purple.

Illustrated by Kelly Kennedy

Rhyme Time

Can you match each definition with the pair of rhyming words it describes? You'll have fun before you're done!

1. Tool from Paris — h. French wrench
2. A do-nothing flower — a. Jelly deli
3. Chocolate at the beach — b. Mountain fountain
4. High-altitude geyser — c. Muddy buddy
5. Spilled OJ — d. Lazy daisy
6. Athlete's footwear — e. Green queen
7. Jam store — f. Morning warning
8. Seasick royalty — 1 / g. Dove glove
9. Alarm clock — h. French wrench
10. Dirty friend — i. Loose juice
11. Bird's baseball mitt — j. Quick lick
12. A tiny lollipop — k. Sandy candy
— l. Jock sock

Puzzle by Denise Stanley and Pam Webb

Illustrated by Dave Clegg

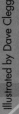

SCRAMBLERS

Six animals that people might keep as pets are hidden in these letters. To find out what they are, first find each group of letters that look the same. Then unscramble each group to name a type of pet.

O Z R S D H A R B D

O R T I D B E

D I T H G R P I E

T G A S O L A T

L F O L R I O

B A M R

1 _____

2 _____

3 _____

4 _____

5 _____

6 _____

99

This and That

Some things just go together, like peanut butter and jelly. Every answer in this crossword includes two things that are often linked. Start and finish the puzzle if you can!

Across

1. Peanut butter and ___
3. Milk and ___
5. Goofus and ___
9. Husband and ___
10. Salt and ___
11. Macaroni and ___
15. Hansel and ___
16. Soap and ___
18. Bacon and ___
20. Spaghetti and ___
23. Bits and ___
24. Needle and ___
25. Rock and ___

Down

1. Jack and ___
2. Cats and ___
3. Arts and ___
4. Sticks and ___
6. Thunder and ___
7. Tweedledee and ___
8. King and ___
12. Sugar and ___
13. Romeo and ___
14. Lewis and ___
17. Show and ___
19. Shoes and ___
21. Bow and ___
22. Bread and ___
23. Pencil and ___

Illustrated by Hey Kids!

Y's Words

Can you find **17** different Y words hidden in this grid? They are hidden up, down, across, backwards, and diagonally.

Word List

~~YAHOO~~   YEAR   YOGA
YAK   YELLOW   YOGURT
~~YAM~~   YESTERDAY   YOLK
YARD   YET   YOUNG
~~YARN~~   YO-YO   YOUR
~~YAWN~~   YODEL

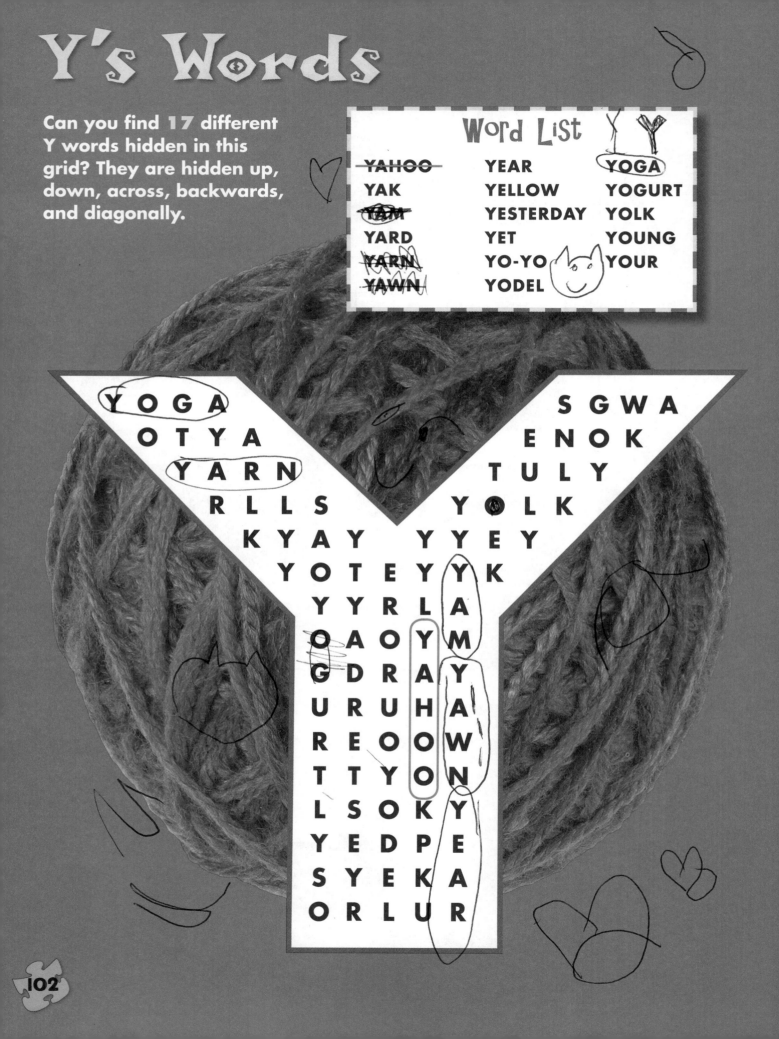

```
Y O G A              S G W A
O T Y A              E N O K
Y A R N          T U L Y
R L L S          Y O L K
K Y A Y        Y Y E Y
Y O T E Y    Y Y K
Y Y R L Y A M
O A O Y A M
G D R A Y A
U R U H O A W
R E O O N
T T Y O K Y
L S O K P E
Y E D P E A
S Y E K A
O R L U R
```

Word for Words

The letters in **HIPPOPOTAMUS** can be used to make many other words. Use the clues below to come up with some of them. A type of meat, for example, might make you think of the word HAM. See how many of the others you can guess.

HIPPOPOTAMUS

1. A type of meat __H A M__
2. The sound of a breaking balloon __POP__
3. A beanie, beret, or bowler __HAT__
4. A common red road sign __STOP__
5. This takes you on a voyage. __SHIP__
6. A slam dunk goes through this. __ __ __ __ __
7. Chicken noodle is a type of this. __SOUP__
8. A way to prepare potatoes __MASH__
9. To look for something to buy __SHOP__
10. Junk e-mail __SPAM__
11. A horse eats these. __OATS__
12. The sound an owl makes __WOO O__
13. You chew food in it. __ __ __ __ __
14. To spray water like a whale __SPOUT__
15. The opposite of rough __SMOOTH__

Can you find the hidden objects that start with SH?

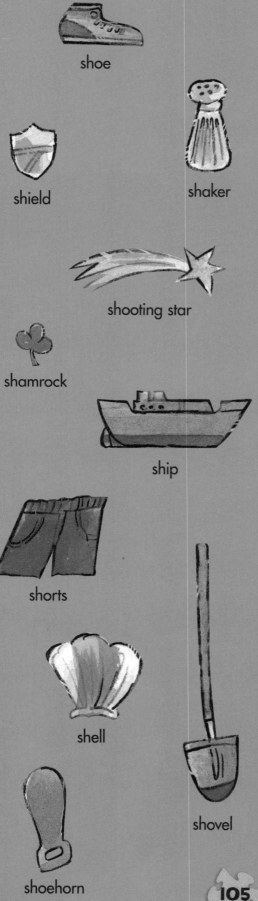

shoe

shield

shaker

shooting star

shamrock

ship

shorts

shell

shovel

shoehorn

CHAMPIONSHIP CHALLENGE

Check this out! Take a closer look. There are at least **33** things that begin with the letters **CH**. How many can you chase down?

Illustrated by David Coulson

Fruit Sudoku

Each of these grids holds one type of fruit. Fill in the boxes so that each row, column, and 6-letter section contains the letters of that fruit. We've filled in some of the letters to get you started. Can you fill in the rest?

ORANGE

O	R	A	N	G	E
E		G			
			R		G
R			A		G
N	E	O		R	
G	A		E		O

GRAPES

G	R	A	P	E	S
	P	E		A	G
	G		A		
	A				E
A	S			R	
		P	G	S	A

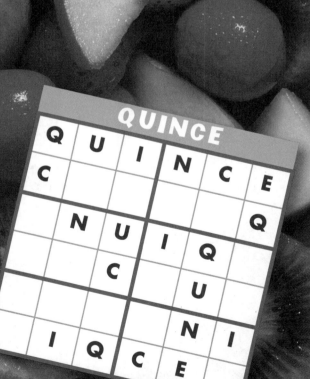

QUINCE

Q	U	I	N	C	E
C				C	E
	N	U	I	Q	
		C		U	
				N	I
	I	Q	C	C	E

Each of these clues will lead you to a word or a phrase. You just have to look at them in the right way. How many can you name?

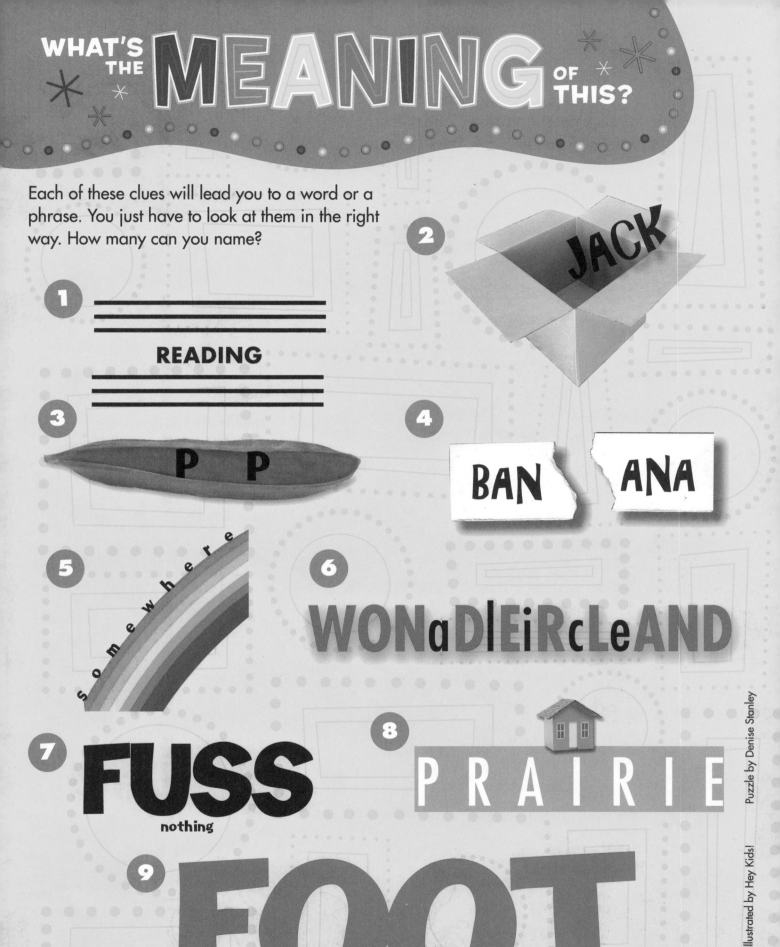

1 READING

2 JACK

3 P P

4 BAN ANA

5 somewhere

6 WONaDlEiRcLeAND

7 FUSS nothing

8 PRAIRIE

9 FOOT

Puzzle by Denise Stanley

Illustrated by Hey Kids!

109

Surf to Turf

Sal is going for his longest ride ever. Can you find the one path that will take him safely back to shore?

Start

Finish

110

BONUS PUZZLE

Did you find the path? Now write all the letters you found on it, in order, in the spaces below. They'll answer the riddle.

Where does an amoeba surf?

__ __ __ __ __ __ __ __ __

Illustrated by Ron Zalme

III

Stop, Look, and List

Are you ready for a trivia challenge? Fill in each box with a name or word. It must begin with the letter at the top of the column. We put in a few of our favorites to get you started.

	S	T	O	P
Girls' Names				
Made-Up Words	Shnibble			
Fruits or Veggies				
Computer Words		Toolbar		
Sea Creatures				Pufferfish
Silly Kinds of Cookies			Old Sweatsock Chip	
Colors	Silver			
States				

Hidden Pairs

Each pair of words below is hiding something. Look closely and you'll find a pair of shorter but related words in the original pair. For example, in the first pair you can find **MOM** and **DAD**. Can you find the other hidden pairs?

1. **mom**ent, doo**dad**

2. struck, cargo

3. badger, goodbye

4. diving, shout

5. charm, bubblegum

6. history, sherbet

7. clover, thunder

8. sunken, honeymoon

9. grunt, boardwalk

10. rocket, stroll

11. frightened, leftovers

12. shower, constellation

Illustrated by Kelly Kennedy

GOING IN CIRCLES

1. Hot-fudge dessert
6. Opposite of full
10. The yellow of an egg
13. A baby cat
18. Short time of sleep
20. A "pie" with cheese
24. Similar to a crocodile
32. "_____ and shine!"
35. Our home planet
39. Pumps oxygen to the body
43. Big brass instrument
46. Not multiplication, division, or subtraction
53. Five cents
58. A large spotted cat
64. A double-_____ bus
69. Smallest state in the U.S.
79. Rumba, salsa, or tap
83. Opposite of begin
85. Snare or bass
88. St. Patrick's Day month
92. Sport with a puck
97. Japanese money
99. Direction a compass points
103. A kind of crab
108. Things you floss
112. Opposite of good-bye

Around and around you'll go! Use the clues to fill in the spaces below. This is like a regular crossword puzzle, but with one twist: the last letter of each word will also be the first letter of the next word. Use those linking letters as hints to figure out the right words.

Puzzle by Carly Schuna

Illustrated by Jim Steck

Music Q's

Missing Vowels

SNG TTLS are the words *song titles* with the vowels taken away. Can you figure out the names of these five **SNG TTLS?**

_____
TH STR-SPNGLD BNNR

_____
HPPY BRTHDY T Y

_____
JNGL BLLS

_____
YNK DDL

_____
TK M T T TH BLL GM

Brass or Wind?

Some of these are brass instruments and others are woodwinds. Can you figure out which is which?

TRUMPET
CLARINET
FLUTE
TROMBONE
TUBA
SAXOPHONE
BUGLE
OBOE
PICCOLO
BARITONE HORN

Guess What?

Can you figure out what these two instruments are?

Piano Path

Lina is late for her piano lesson. Can you help her get there on time?

Start →

Finish

Illustrated by Mike Moran

TWiN Guitars

Which two guitars are exactly alike?

A

B

C

D

JUMBLed MUSiC

Unscramble each set of letters to get a type of music.

ZAZJ ___ ___ ___ ___

PHI POH ___ ___ ___ ___ ___ ___

REAPO ___ ___ ___ ___ ___

TRONUCY ___ ___ ___ ___ ___ ___ ___

CORK DAN LORL ___ ___ ___ ___ ___ ___ ___ ___ ___ ___ ___

117

Each of these clues will lead you to a sports team or expression. You just need to look at them in the right way. How many can you name?

1. F*IRST ↓

2. SHOT SHOT SHOT SHOT GOAL

3. 1

4. STOP

5. GAME

6. COUNT

7. LIBERTY LIBERTY LIBERTY

8. THE PLAY

9. FIELD

Hidden Pictures® Book Lovers

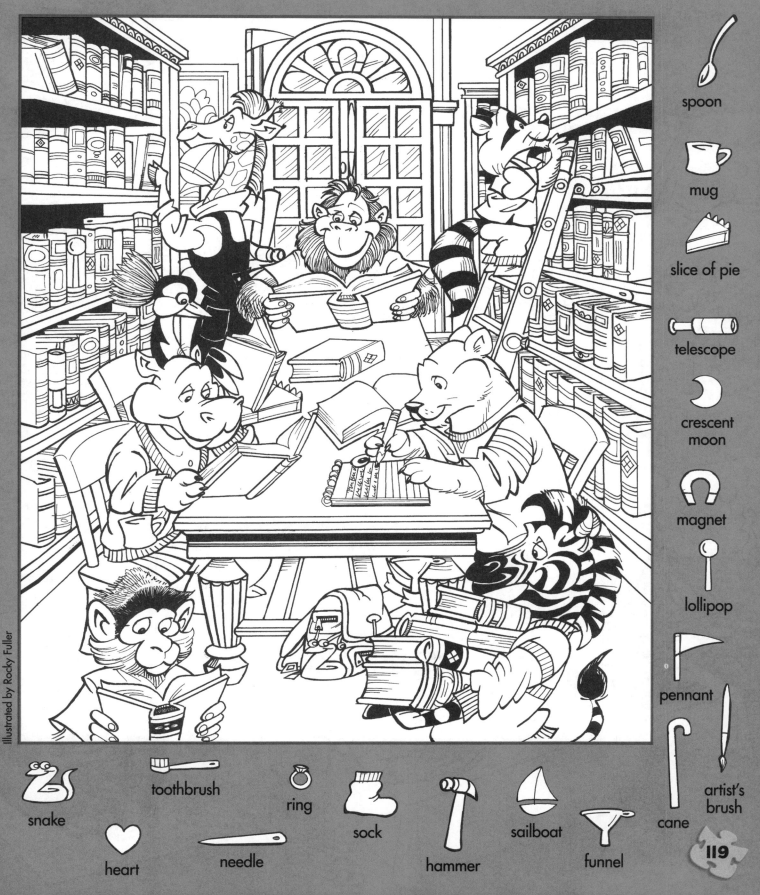

Illustrated by Rocky Fuller

spoon

mug

slice of pie

telescope

crescent moon

magnet

lollipop

pennant

cane

artist's brush

snake

heart

toothbrush

needle

ring

sock

hammer

sailboat

funnel

119

Seeing Doubles

Calling all puzzlers! Take a good look around. There are at least **40** things whose names contain double letters—like ball and pizza. How many other double-letter words do you see?

DAN'S DINER

TRY 10

1. Name three things you use your feet to do.

2. Which sport uses the smallest ball?
○ golf ○ baseball ○ tennis

3. Name four things you might keep in your pocket.

4. The Atlantic Ocean is next to California.
○ True ○ False

CALIFORNIA

PET SHOP

5. The word "gato" is Spanish for which animal?
○ dog ○ cat ○ bird

6. Name three words that rhyme with "flea."

7. Emerald, olive, and jade are shades of what color?

8. Circle the animal that eats plants.

9. Kids usually have 100 baby teeth.
○ True   ○ False

10. Which is twice as much as 9?

Illustrated by Kelly Kennedy

Say What?

Texting Tessie loves to be brief. To her, there are 60 S in a M. That's 60 seconds in a minute to the rest of us. Can you figure out some more of Tessie's shortcuts?

1. 60 S in a M <u>**60 seconds in a minute**</u>

2. 7 D in a W _____

3. 12 I in a F _____

4. 12 M in a Y _____

5. 4 Q in a G _____

6. 2 C in a P _____

7. 60 M in an H _____

8. 3 F in a Y _____

9. 24 H in a D _____

10. 26 L in the A _____

11. 52 W in a Y _____

12. 365 D in a Y _____

13. 100 Y in a C _____

14. 52 C in a D _____

15. 50 S on the U.S. F _____

124

Double Cross

To "work out" the answer to the riddle below, first cross out all the pairs of matching letters. Then write the remaining letters in order in the spaces next to the riddle.

QQ EE BB JU MM OO WW
LL MP SS VV YY ZZ IN
II AA RR NN EE GF YY
HH XX PP DD LA UU SS
GG OO PJ SS CC QQ II
CC YY EE MM AA TT AC
UU BB KK VV ZZ KS TT

What kind of exercises do pancakes do?

_ _ _ _ _ _ _
_ _ _ _ _ _ _ _

125

Recycle It!

Arun is headed to the recycling center. On the way, he has to pick up three bags of things to recycle. Can you help him reach each item and unscramble its name? Once you've got each one, continue along the path until you get to the center. Just one path will take you from **START** to **FINISH**.

Start

SNAPPEREW

Illustrated by Steve Skelton

CLASTIP

ROADDCRAB

Finish

Dive IN

Alex, Brooke, and Claire are competing in the big race. Who will win? Find out by answering these questions. For each question, circle the answer listed under **A**, **B**, or **C**, Then shade in the matching square in the correct swim lane. As you do, the swimmers will cruise to the finish line. Can you guess which girl will finish first?

Which is ...

 A   **B**   **C**

	A	B	C
1. a fruit with a pit?	apple	apricot	strawberry
2. a baby goat?	kid	fawn	cygnet
3. the Labor Day month?	January	July	September
4. part of a whale's body?	scales	armor	blubber
5. a metric measurement?	inch	centimeter	mile
6. a type of rock?	gumbo	gaucho	granite
7. a shade of red?	scarlet	tawny	emerald
8. the world's tallest mountain?	Everest	Kilimanjaro	Denali
9. what a plant makes?	colonel	chlorine	chlorophyll
10. a kind of poem?	cornet	sonnet	gazette
11. the language of Chile?	Spanish	Italian	Korean
12. a mythical creature?	wildebeest	dodo	unicorn
13. the "serve and volley" sport?	tennis	water polo	bowling
14. the state with St. Paul as its capital?	Kentucky	Minnesota	New Mexico
15. the shape with the most sides?	triangle	pentagon	trapezoid
16. what "jovial" means?	happy	confused	upset
17. a German city?	Bangkok	Belfast	Berlin
18. the number of feet in a mile?	1,460	5,280	10,000
19. what an entomologist studies?	ghosts	fossils	insects
20. the age of a centenarian?	90	75	100

A

B

C

Wh@+'s f0® D!nne®?

NACHOS

N@©h0$ _____

B33f +@©0$ _____

©h!ck3n Bu®®!+0 _____

©h33$3 3n©h!1@d@ _____

W0n+0n $0up _____

P0®k f®!3d r!©3 _____

P3k!ng du©k _____

F0®+un3 ©00k!3$ _____

@n+!p@$+0 _____

B@k3d Z!+! _____

®@v!01! w!+h M3@+ $@uc3 _____

©h!©k3n P@®m3$@n _____

M!$0 $0up _____

uh! D31ux3 _____

©h!ck3n +3®!y@k! _____

$hr!mp +3mpu®@ _____

130

Hidden Pictures®
Go Team!

wishbone

bagel

fork

binoculars

banana

glove

baseball bat

saltshaker

hockey puck

ruler

crescent moon

ring

pitchfork

horseshoe

Illustrated by Dave Clegg

131

Mail Call!

This postal carrier has one last letter to deliver today. Can you help him find the path to the mailbox? When you're done, write the letters along the route in the spaces below to answer the riddle.

Start

Finish

What is the best kind of letter to read on a hot day?

__ __ __ __   __ __ __ __ __

Illustrated by Jim Paillot

5 Word for Words

1. EMU
2. BUS
3. RAM
4. BARN
5. NEAR
6. RAIN
7. MANE
8. BEAM
9. MINUS
10. SIREN
11. NURSE
12. NUMBER

8–9 Comic Shop

11 Weight a Second!

14–15 Scuba Time

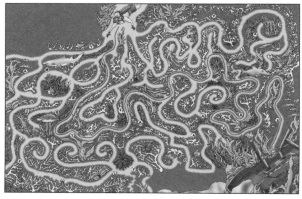

How do you say good-bye to the ocean?
YOU WAVE!

6–7 Zany Z Puzzle

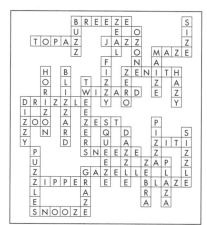

10 What's the Meaning of This?

1. One in a Million
2. Repeat After Me
3. Long Underwear
4. Just in Case
5. Head Over Heels
6. Square Dance
7. Hole in One
8. Crossroads

12–13 Time to Rhyme

16 Nice to See You!

133

Answers

17 Double Cross

What does bread do when it is baked with shoe polish?

IT RISES AND SHINES.

18-19 Ring the Bell

1. B	6. B	11. C	16. C
2. B	7. C	12. A	17. B
3. A	8. A	13. B	18. B
4. C	9. C	14. B	19. C
5. A	10. A	15. C	20. C

C rings the bell.

22 Alphabet Soup

24-25 Hilarious!

20-21 From A to Z

artist	jump rope	swing
bridge	kangaroo	turtle
crown	lobster	umbrella
drum	mustache	valentine
egg	nest	whale
fence	ostrich	xylophone
guitar	pelican	yarn
hippopotamus	queen	zebra
ice-cream cone	rooster	

23 Sudoku Garden

VIOLET

V	O	I	L	E	T
T	L	E	V	I	O
I	V	L	O	T	E
O	E	T	I	V	L
L	T	V	E	O	I
E	I	O	T	L	V

ORCHID

H	D	C	O	R	I
I	O	R	D	C	H
R	H	I	C	O	D
O	C	D	I	H	R
C	I	H	R	D	O
D	R	O	H	I	C

CLOVER

E	R	O	L	V	C
V	C	L	R	O	E
C	L	R	O	E	V
O	E	V	C	R	L
R	V	C	E	L	O
L	O	E	V	C	R

26 What's for Breakfast?

- Bacon and eggs
- Toasted English muffin
- Blueberry pancakes
- Waffles
- Orange juice
- Oatmeal with brown sugar
- Whole wheat toast
- French toast
- Cold cereal with milk
- Scrambled eggs
- Bagel with cream cheese
- Vanilla yogurt
- Cinnamon rolls
- Hash brown potatoes
- Breakfast burrito

27 Box Drops

1. WHAT GAME DO SHARKS LIKE TO PLAY? SWALLOW THE LEADER

2. HOW DO WHALES TIE UP THEIR PONYTAILS? WITH BLUBBER BANDS

28–29 Try 10

1. Basketball, baseball, and bowling. Did you think of others?
2. Mice, dice, and ice
3. Circle the cucumber.
4. A photograph is about to be taken.
5. True
6. Museum
7. To get someone's attention and to get past a person blocking the way
8. Canada, Brazil, Denmark, and Japan
9. May
10. Circle the vine on the right.

32–33 Game Q's

Go Seek!

Fair Game

If someone has done work in advance, she is ahead of the game. **T**

If someone has got game it means he's not very talented. **F**

If a store is the only game in town, it means it has mini-golf. **F**

If someone has a game plan, he has a strategy in place. **T**

Missing Vowels

TAG
HORSESHOES
HOPSCOTCH
FOLLOW THE LEADER
CAPTURE THE FLAG

Chess or Not?

Queen
Rook
Bishop
Pawn
Knight
King

A Pair of Jacks

36 All Talk

30–31 Ready, Set, Grow!

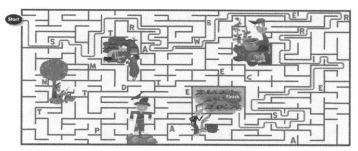

What is a scarecrow's favorite fruit?
STRAWBERRIES

34–35 Going in Circles

1. GIRAFFE	51. TOMATO
7. ENTER	56. OUT
11. RAT	58. TEXAS
13. THRONE	62. SUGAR
18. EIGHT	66. RATTLE
22. TRAIL	71. ELBOW
26. LUNCH	75. WHITE
30. HISS	79. EASY
33. SOCCER	82. YESTERDAY
38. RAISIN	90. YOUNG
43. NEW YORK	94. GOOD-BYE
49. KIT	

37 Hieroglyphs

Answers

38 Good Fortune

SMILE! YOU ARE ONE SMART COOKIE!

39 Animal Tricks

1. CAT	2. WORM	3. GOAT	4. DUCK
COT	WORE	MOAT	DOCK
DOT	WIRE	MOAN	SOCK
DOG	WISE	MOON	SOAK
	WISH	LOON	SOAR
	FISH	LION	SCAR
			SCAN
			SWAN

40–41 Great Grilling

42 Stop, Look, and List

Here's what we thought of. You may have thought of others.

Boys' Names: Sean, Thomas, Omar, Pierre

Sandwich Ingredients: salami, tomato, onions, peanut butter

Words with LL in Them: silly, tall, overall, pollywog

Halloween Costumes: sorcerer, tiger, ogre, princess

Silly Ice-Cream Flavors: string bean, taco chip, okra, peppercorn

Birds: sea gull, turkey, owl, penguin

Cities: Seattle, WA; Tampa, FL; Oakland, CA; Pittsburgh, PA

Baseball Words: shortstop, triple, out, pitcher

43 Scrambled Birds

DOVE	ROBIN	PIGEON	PENGUIN
CROW	STORK	PARROT	FLAMINGO
HAWK	GOOSE	SPARROW	CARDINAL
SWAN			

Why do hummingbirds hum?
BECAUSE THEY DON'T KNOW THE WORDS.

44–45 Cut It Out!

What do fishermen plant in their lawns?
CRABGRASS

46–47 SwEEt!

bee	freezer	pinwheel	street
beet	geese	queen	sweep
beetle	green	reel	tee
cartwheel	Halloween	referee	tepee
cheerleader	knee	screen	teeth
cheese	leek	seeds	three
coffee	needle	sheep	tree
deer	parakeet	sheet	tweezers
eel	peek	sleep	weed
feet	peel	speedboat	wheel
			wheelbarrow

48 Kiddie Ride

What do babies ride at amusement parks?
STROLLER COASTERS

49 Chinatown

50–51 X Marks the Spot

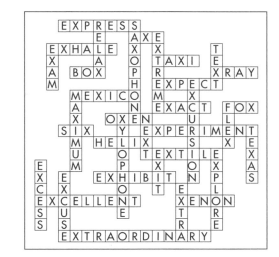

52–53 Metro Map

54 Pencil Paths

55 What's for Lunch?

SOUPS

French onion
Beef barley
Chicken noodle
Clam chowder
Cream of mushroom
Split pea with ham

SANDWICHES

Bacon, lettuce, and tomato
Egg salad
Grilled cheese
Ham and cheese
Peanut butter and jelly
Pulled pork
Roast beef
Tuna melt
Turkey club

56–57 Catch You Later!

Answers

58–59 Flower Power

60 Double Cross

Why are cats good at video games?
THEY ALL HAVE NINE LIVES.

61 See You Later, Galilator

1. crocodile
2. baboon
3. buffalo
4. sheep
5. gecko
6. butterfly
7. kangaroo
8. polar bear
9. chimpanzee
10. rattlesnake

62–63 Fantastic Gymnastics

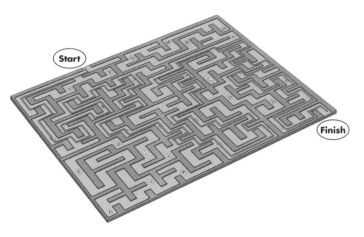

How do gymnasts feel after a routine?
HEAD OVER HEELS

64–65 Everything Is OK!

Here are some words we found.
You may have found others.

Oak	Organ	Kick
Oar	Ostrich	Kilt
Oboe	Otter	King
O'clock	Oven	Kiss
Octopus	Oven mitt	Kitchen
Olive	Owl	Kite
Omelet	Oyster	Kitten
One	Kangaroo	Knee
Onion	Kayak	Knife
Opossum	Kazoo	Knight
Orange	Ketchup	Knob
Orca	Kettle	Knock
Orchid	Key	Knot
	Keyboard	

66 Spelling Bee

67 Mixed Nuts Sudoku

ALMOND					
A	L	M	O	N	D
D	O	N	L	M	A
N	A	D	M	O	L
O	M	L	D	A	N
M	D	A	N	L	O
L	N	O	A	D	M

PEANUT					
P	E	A	N	U	T
T	N	U	P	A	E
A	P	N	E	T	U
E	U	T	A	P	N
N	T	P	U	E	A
U	A	E	T	N	P

CASHEW					
C	A	S	H	E	W
E	W	H	A	S	C
W	H	A	S	C	E
S	C	E	W	A	H
A	E	W	C	H	S
H	S	C	E	W	A

138

68–69 Eek!

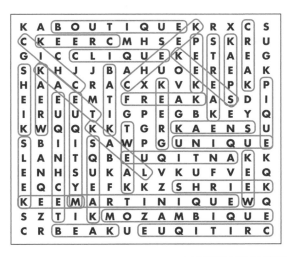

72 Box Drops

1.

2.

70–71 Do the Opposite

73 A Tree Stumper

WALNUT BIRCH OAK
CHERRY MAPLE HICKORY
PINE   CEDAR DOGWOOD
      WILLOW

The world's tallest species of tree is
THE REDWOOD.

74–75 Flowers and Flamingoes

76–77 Pizza Path

Parker does not like salt.
So what will he order on his pizza?
PEPPER ONLY

78–79 Shhhhhhhh!

Answers

80 Q Cross

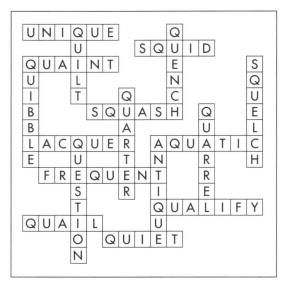

81 Teaching T

82–83 Strange!

Here are the ST words we found.
You may have found others.

stack	station	stool	strawberry
stadium	statue	stop sign	stream
stage	steak	store	street
stairs	stegosaurus	stork	string
stamp	stick	storm	stripes
stapler	stilts	story	strongman
star	stingray	stove	student
starfish	stone	straw	stump

84–85 T Party

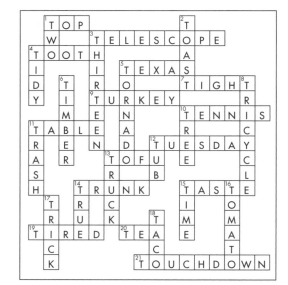

86 Fish Tales

87 What's the Word?

1. A panini is a type of sandwich.
2. A pollywog is a tadpole.
3. A frock is a dress.
4. A minnow is a small fish.
5. A marina is a place to dock boats.
6. A cygnet is a baby swan.
7. A dollop is a small portion.
8. An anaconda is a snake.
9. A quetzal is a bird.
10. A ziggurat is an ancient pyramid.

Answers

88–89 Swim Meet

Where do minivans go swimming?
IN A CARPOOL

91 A Key Clue

You must search the island. Find five keys hidden in the picture. They will open the locks on the treasure chest.

94–95 B All You Can B

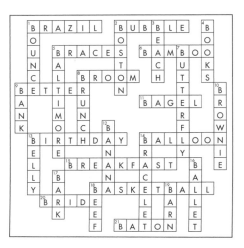

90 Word for Words

1. SEA
2. BUS
3. BELL
4. MARS
5. MEAL
6. BALL
7. BEAR
8. EARS
9. MULE
10. BLUE
11. SAME
12. SMELL
13. LUMBER
14. SMALLER
15. MARBLES

92–93 Up and Down

96–97 Try 10

1. Circle the E.
2. 24 inches
3. Leopard and cheetah
   Did you think of others?
4. Three months—January, June, and July
5. Texas
6. Goat, boat, and note
7. Apple pie, apple sauce, and apple juice
8. Circle letter on the right.
9. False
10. Plums and violets

98 Rhyme Time

1—h 4—b 7—a 10—c
2—d 5—i 8—e 11—g
3—k 6—l 9—f 12—j

141

Answers

99 Scramblers

1. DOG
2. RABBIT
3. LIZARD
4. PARROT
5. HAMSTER
6. GOLDFISH

102 Y's Words

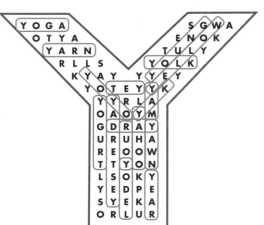

100–101 This and That

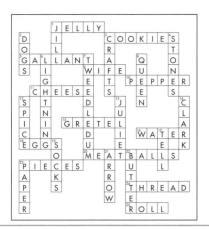

103 Word for Words

1. HAM
2. POP
3. HAT
4. STOP
5. SHIP
6. HOOP
7. SOUP
8. MASH
9. SHOP
10. SPAM
11. OATS
12. HOOT
13. MOUTH
14. SPOUT
15. SMOOTH

104–105 Shower Time

106–107 Championship Challenge

Here are some words we found.
You may have found others.

chain	chariot	chessboard	chimney
chainsaw	chart	chest	chimpanzee
chair	check	chew	chipmunk
chairlift	checkbook	chick	chips
chalk	checkers	chicken	chirp
chalkboard	cheerleaders	chief	chisel
champion	cheese	children	chocolate
change	cheetah	chili	chopsticks
charcoal	cherry	chili pepper	church

108 Fruit Sudoku

GRAPES

G	R	A	P	E	S
S	P	E	R	A	G
E	G	S	A	P	R
P	A	R	S	G	E
A	S	G	E	R	P
R	E	P	G	S	A

ORANGE

O	R	A	N	G	E
E	N	G	O	A	R
A	O	N	R	E	G
R	G	E	A	O	N
N	E	O	G	R	A
G	A	R	E	N	O

QUINCE

Q	U	I	N	C	E
C	E	N	U	I	Q
E	N	U	I	Q	C
I	Q	C	E	U	N
U	C	E	Q	N	I
N	I	Q	C	E	U

109 What's the Meaning of This?

1. Reading between the lines
2. Jack-in-the-box
3. Two peas in a pod
4. Banana split
5. Somewhere over the rainbow
6. Alice in Wonderland
7. Big fuss over nothing
8. Little House on the Prairie
9. Bigfoot

110–111 Surf to Turf

Where does an amoeba surf?
ON A MICROWAVE

112 Stop, Look, and List

Here's what we thought of.
You may have thought of others.
Girls' Names: Sydney, Tisha, Olivia, Paula
Made-Up Words: Shnibble, Ticktoo, Oogie, Pluffff
Fruits or Veggies: Spinach, Tomato, Orange, Peach
Computer Words: Search, Toolbar, Online, Print
Sea Creatures: Squid, Tuna, Octopus, Pufferfish
Silly Kinds of Cookies: Spinach Raisin, Turkey Chocolate, Old Sweatsock Chip, Parmesan Cheese Crunch
Colors: Silver, Turquoise, Orange, Pink
States: South Dakota, Texas, Ohio, Pennsylvania

113 Hidden Pairs

1. mom, dad
2. truck, car
3. bad, good
4. in, out
5. arm, leg
6. his, her
7. over, under
8. sun, moon
9. run, walk
10. rock, roll
11. right, left
12. show, tell

114–115 Going in Circles

1. SUNDAE
6. EMPTY
10. YOLK
13. KITTEN
18. NAP
20. PIZZA
24. ALLIGATOR
32. RISE
35. EARTH
39. HEART
43. TUBA
46. ADDITION
53. NICKEL
58. LEOPARD
64. DECKER
69. RHODE ISLAND
79. DANCE
83. END
85. DRUM
88. MARCH
92. HOCKEY
97. YEN
99. NORTH
103. HERMIT
108. TEETH
112. HELLO

116–117 Music Q's

Missing Vowels

THE STAR-SPANGLED BANNER

HAPPY BIRTHDAY TO YOU

JINGLE BELLS

YANKEE DOODLE

TAKE ME OUT TO THE BALL GAME

Brass or Wind?

Brass: trumpet, trombone, tuba, bugle, baritone horn

Woodwind: clarinet, flute, saxophone, oboe, piccolo

Jumbled Music

JAZZ
HIP HOP
OPERA
COUNTRY
ROCK AND ROLL

Guess What?

saxophone   drum set

Piano Path

Twin Guitars

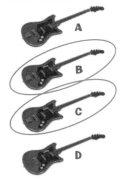

118 What's the Meaning of This?

1. First Down
2. Shots on Goal
3. Hole in One
4. Shortstop
5. All-Star Game
6. Full Count
7. Third Quarter
8. Flag on the Play
9. Taking the Field

119 Book Lovers

143

Answers

120–121 Seeing Doubles
Here are some words we found. You may have found others.

apples	bottle	collar	giraffe	kitten	pepper mill	rattle	swimmer
arrow	bubble	cook	glass	ladder	peppermint	ribbon	tools
ball	buffalo	creek	goggles	lasso	sticks	roof	tree
balloon	butter	doll	goose	letter	pizza	saddle	tunnel
banana peel	butterfly	door	gorilla	lettuce	poodle	sheep	umbrella
barrel	caboose	dress	grass	lollipop	pool	slippers	well
bees	carrot	eel	grill	mirror	propeller	spoon	wheel
beetle	caterpillar	eggs	hammer	mitt	puddle	squirrel	wood
billy goat	cell phone	falls	hill	moose	puppies	stool	
book	cherry	fiddle	hippo	mushrooms	rabbit	strawberries	
boots	coffee	flippers	juggler	paddle	raccoon	stroller	

122–123 Try 10

1. Dance, jump, and kick. Did you think of others?
2. Golf
3. Keys, wallet, tissues, and a coin
4. False
5. Cat
6. Tree, knee, and three
7. Green
8. Circle the rabbit.
9. False
10. 18

124 Say What?

1. 60 seconds in a minute
2. 7 days in a week
3. 12 inches in a foot
4. 12 months in a year
5. 4 quarts in a gallon
6. 2 cups in a pint
7. 60 minutes in an hour
8. 3 feet in a yard
9. 24 hours in a day
10. 26 letters in the alphabet
11. 52 weeks in a year
12. 365 days in a year
13. 100 years in a century
14. 52 cards in a deck
15. 50 stars on the U.S. flag

125 Double Cross

What kind of exercises do pancakes do?
JUMPING FLAPJACKS

128–129 Dive In

1. B	6. C	11. A	16. A
2. A	7. A	12. C	17. C
3. C	8. A	13. A	18. B
4. C	9. C	14. B	19. C
5. B	10. B	15. B	20. C

Claire (C) wins the race.

126–127 Recycle It!

NEWSPAPER, PLASTIC, CARDBOARD

130 What's for Dinner?

Nachos
Beef Tacos
Chicken Burrito
Cheese Enchilada
Wonton Soup

Pork Fried Rice
Peking Duck
Fortune Cookies
Antipasto
Baked Ziti
Ravioli with
    Meat Sauce

Chicken Parmesan
Miso Soup
Sushi Deluxe
Chicken Teriyaki
Shrimp Tempura

131 Go Team!

132 Mail Call!

Start
Finish

What is the best kind of letter to read on a hot day?
FAN MAIL